SWU-MED-003

NUREMBERG TOURNAMENTS 1446-1561

Luca Stefano Cristini

SOLDIERSHOP PUBLISHING

THE AUTHOR

Luca Stefano Cristini has edited various publications on ancient and contemporary historical themes, including books on thirty years war, Medieval, Napoleonic as well as several illustrated books with historical color photographs. He has also curated all the brands of Soldiershop publishing.

PUBLISHING'S NOTES

LICENSES COMMONS

ACKNOWLEDGEMENTS

A Special Thanks to New York The Metropolitan Museum of Art owner of the original of the book thet release the Pd with a licence CCO 1.0 Related all our book series in the same brand we thanks to also all the several institution, museum, library, bibliotecks, public or private collection & athenaeums that with their positive copyright policy about part of his collections, allows us the use of many images present in our books. We remember same of this great World Institutions: New York Public Library, Rara CH, Heidelberg Biblioteck University, Riikmuseum of Amsterdam, Dusseldorf University Library, Polona Library, Herzog August Bibliothek of Wolfenbüttel, Stuttgart Bibliothek, SLUB Dresden, Frankfurt am Main Universitätsbibliothek, Europeana, Wikipedia, and many others...

For a complete list of Soldiershop titles please contact Luca Cristini Editore on our website: www.soldiershop.com or www.cristinieditore.com. E-mail: info@soldiershop.com

Title: **NUREMBERG TOURNAMENTS 1446-1561** By Luca Stefano Cristini.
ISBN code: 978-88-93274166 First edition February 2019 Cover & Art Design: Luca S. Cristini
Published by Luca Cristini Editore for Soldiershop brand via Orio 35/4 - 24050 Zanica (BG) ITALY. www.soldiershop.com

NUREMBERG TOURNAMENTS 1446-1561

LUCA STEFANO CRISTINI

PREFACE

THE MANUSCRIPT OF NUREMBERG TOURNAMENTS AND PARADES 1446-1561

This German *Turnierbuch* manuscript is composed of 112 sheet includes depictions of contestants equipped for various tournaments; a renaissance parade preceding a late form of tournament called a carrousel; This album represent specifically the participants in tournaments known as *Gesellenstrechen*, or bachelors' jousts, held in Nuremberg (Germany) between 1446 and 1561; We find also depictions of pageant sleighs, some of which were used in a parade held in the winter of 1640–41. The illustrations are probably the work of a renaissance artist or a *Briefmaler*, a particular letter painter, who also would have written and embellished official documents and painted rich coats-of-arms.

In many instances, the names of the tournament participants are written above them. They are armed for the *Gestech* (German tournament), the joust fought with blunt lances. This rare *Turnierbuch* such as provide an invaluable record of the jousters' colorful costumes, fanciful crests, and humorous, often satirical emblems that decorated the jouster's shields and horse trappings. This rare manuscript was bought in 1921 by a French collector, and today is part of the MET collection (The Metropolitan Museum of Art of New York).

In appendix we have insert 16 wonderful color plates from the German reprint book of 1918: Hans Burgkmair des Jungeren - Turnierbuch vom 1529.

THE RENAISSANCE TOURNAMENT

Although weapons and armor are more commonly associated with war, they have both been used in other contexts, including hunting, tournaments and parade costume. For the war, weapons and armor must be especially practical, offering maximum protection and functionality without compromising the movement of the body due to excessive weight or inflexible material. The military costume was often decorated, making sure that the decoration did not prevent its usually operation.

The first forms of the tournament were little different from the military exercises, with the fighters using the same equipment they would use in the war. The first specific objects for use in tournaments - such as extra plates for the protection of the throat and hands or blunt spearheads - were introduced around 1300. During the late fourteenth century, equipment such as the shield and the Great Helm were replaced on the battlefield with more sophisticated equipment, but continued to be used in tournaments. This development eventually led to the creation of specialized armor designed exclusively for certain types of tournaments. Equally important was the invention of the crank, a basic reinforcement which, by adding additional pieces and plates, could be adapted for various purposes both on the battlefield and in different types of tournaments.

The symbolic value of weapons and armor was reflected in their use as display objects in tournaments, parades and triumphs and as funeral successes (for example, a grouping of weapons and armor hanging over a knight's grave). During the Renaissance, some of the most sumptuous swords, maces, firearms, shields and armor were made specifically for ceremonial purposes. Sometimes this armor was called ancient or Roman armor. as he remembered in his form the classical idea.

These objects were intended to imitate weapons and armor of the style used by the heroes of classical antiquity and medieval chivalry. Worn or carried in procession or triumph, they were designed to give the wearer the glory and fame, virtues and achievements of those ancient military leaders that the princes and commanders of the Renaissance sought to emulate. Because these devices were not meant to be at risk of damage or loss in battle, many of the functional and protective qualities of "normal" weapons and lightness of armor, practicality and "look" - had been abandoned in favor of the theater and the symbolic effect. Finally, mention must also be made of the armor for the horses and dogs. And above all the horses could be protected or adorned with armor for most of the occasions mentioned above, with sumptuous caparisoned cover, often designed on the occasion by great artists of the time.

Nuremberg in Germany had a cultural flowering in the fifteenth and sixteenth centuries which made it the center of the German Renaissance. In 1525, Nuremberg accepted the Protestant Reformation, and shortly thereafter the religious peace of Nuremberg, with which the Lutherans obtained essential concessions, was signed in Nuremberg. The development of the city grew decisively, acquiring considerable importance throughout Germany. The German Renaissance was a widespread cultural and artistic movement among German thinkers in the fifteenth and sixteenth centuries. Many areas of the arts and sciences were influenced, in particular by the spread of Renaissance humanism in the various German states and principalities. There has been much progress and two developments have dominated the sixteenth century, the press and the Protestant Reformation.

The Nuremberg Turnierbuch (or Album of Tournaments and Parades in Nuremberg) is a German tournament book covering various periods between the mid 16th and mid 17th centuries. The original currently rests in the holdings of Metropolitan Museum of Art in New York City, NY. The Met divides this manuscript into five separate parts; the first is a copy of the tournament book of Hans Burgkmair der Jüngere (plate 1-16), while the other four describe various tournaments and parades held in the city of Nuremberg. It may have been created for the Volckamer family, given the prominence of the exploits of Berthold Volckamer. Created in several stages during the 16th and 17th centuries, possibly copied from older records; the paper dates to the 1530s, while the fourth section describes a parade that occured in 1640 (this last part are present partially in our book). The Nuremberg tournament show in our book is a typical modern carousel emerging from the ancient jousting traditions in Europe. The knights galloped in circles as they threw balls from one to the other. This game was introduced in Europe at the time of the Crusades from previous Eastern traditions. While the first carousels and tournaments were used to prepare and strengthen the knights for a real fight while wielding their weapons.

GLOSSARY OF GERMAN TERMS ABOUT TURNIERBUCH

Ablaufen - running off
Abnehmen - taking off
Abschneiden - cutting off
Absetzen - setting off
Ansetzen - setting on
Duplieren - doubling
Durchgehen / geh durch - go through
Durchwechseln / wechsel durch - change through
Durchlaufen / lauf durch - running through
Eber - guard position, "boar"
Einlaufen - running in
Entrüsthau - hidden strike, "disarming strike"
Geferhau - hidden strike, "danger strike"
Hängen - hanging
Halbhau - "half strike"
Indes - simultaneously, instantly
Langes Messer - long knife
Luginsland - guard position, "look over the land"
Messer - knife

Messernehmen - taking the Messer
Mordschlag - strike with the pommel
Mutieren - mutating
Nachreißen - jerking after
Oberhau - strike from above
Pastei - guard position, "bastion"
Pnehmen / pnimm - removing(?)
Pogen - arc / bow
Schrankhut - "barrier guard"
Sonnenzeigen - showing the sun
Stier - guard position, "bull"
Überlaufen / lauf über - running over
Unterhau - strike from below
Wecker - hidden strike, "wakener"
Winden - winding
Winker - hidden strike, "waver"
Zornhau - hidden strike, "wrath strike"
Zornhau-Ort - Zornhau-point
Zucken - jerking / snatching
Zufechten - approaching in fencing / getting into striking distance / engagement
Zwinger - hidden strike, "forcer"

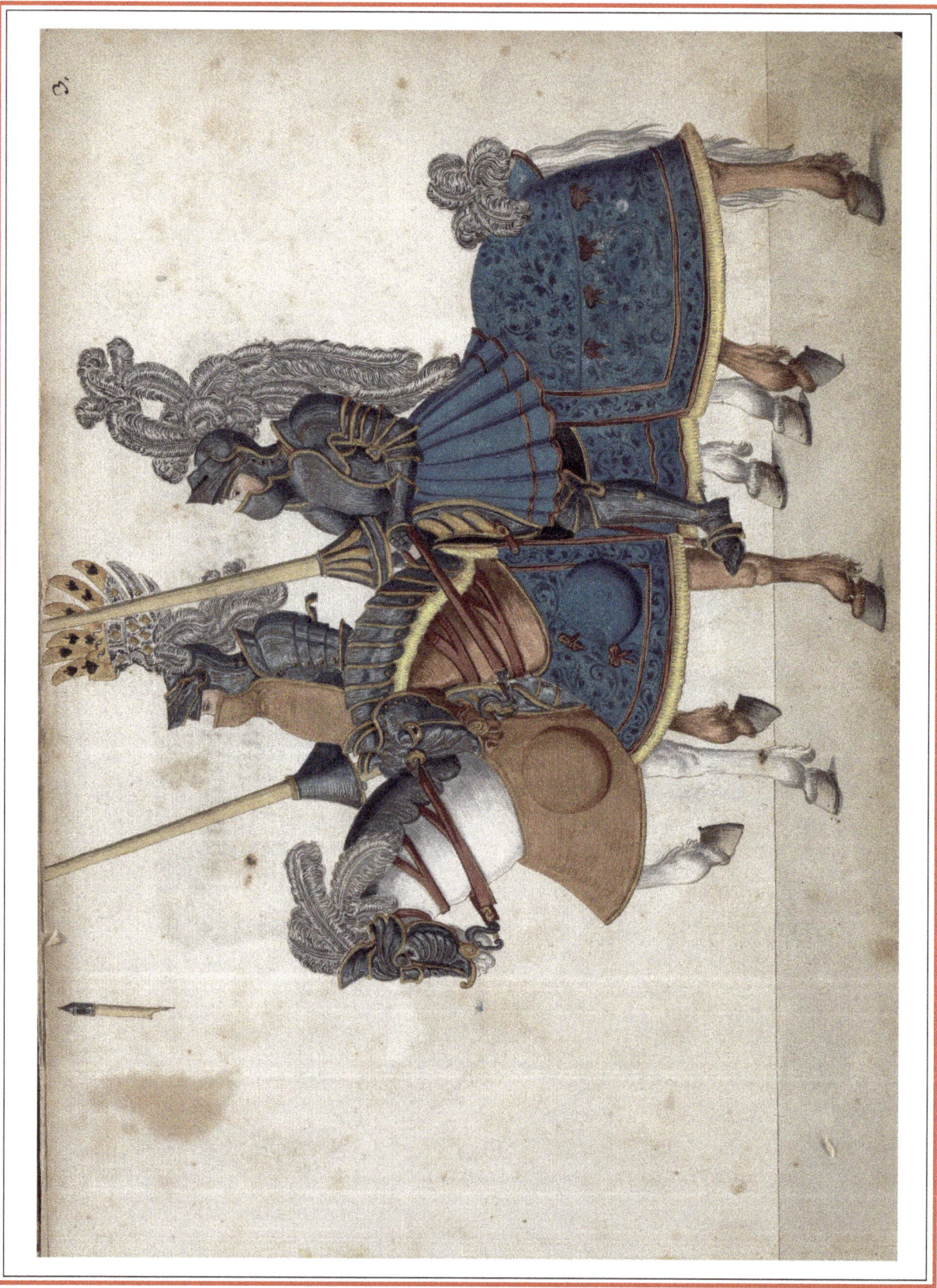

10.

16.

25.

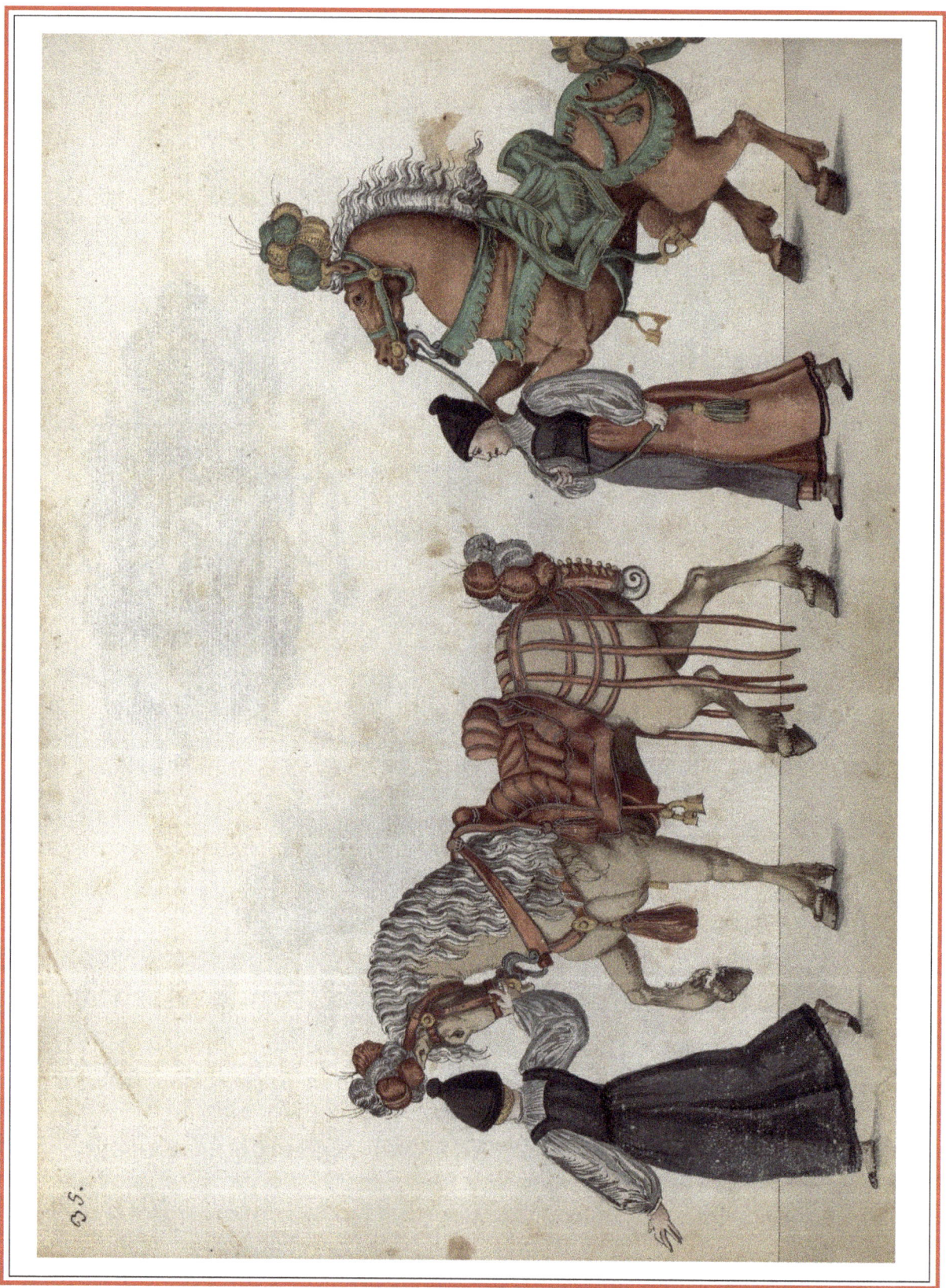

Riſtmaſtr.

40.

41.

Herr Hanns Walbestronner
Hannsen Walbestroners Sohn
von der Grundtherzin geborn.

Conrath Haller Conrath
Hallers vnd der Dandorf-
terin Sohn.

48

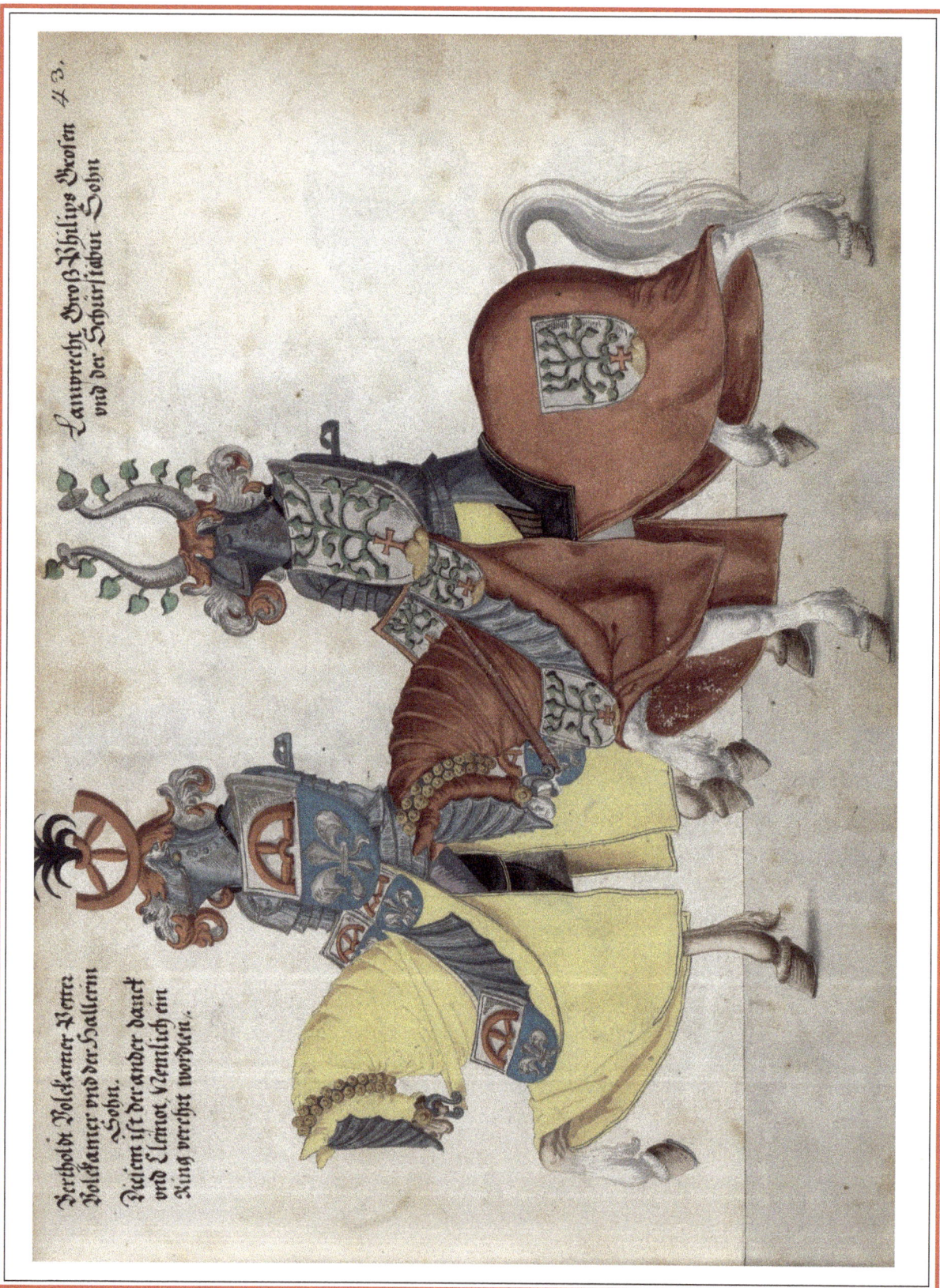

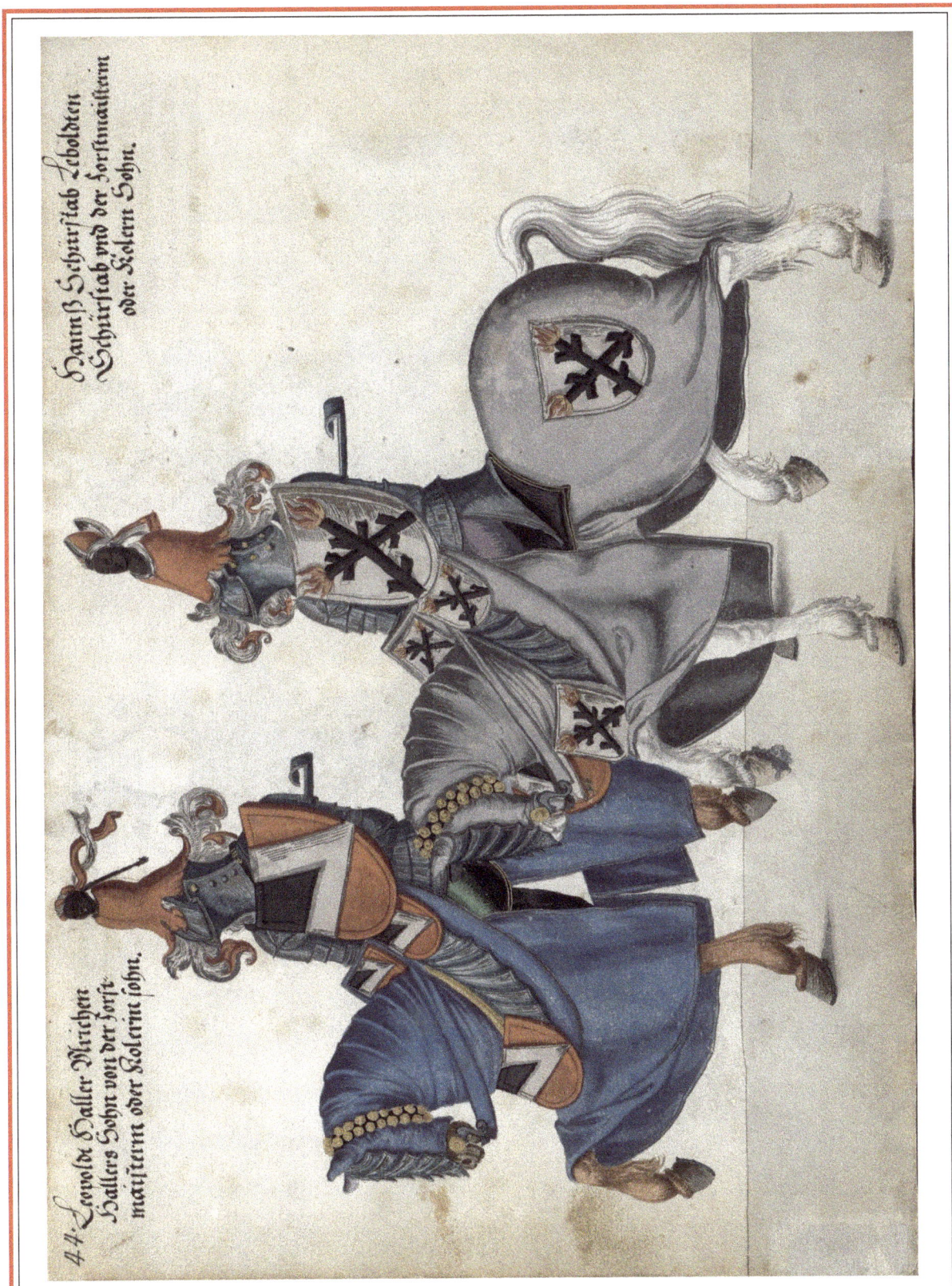

Hanns Schürstab Leboldten
Schürstab vnd der forstmaisterin
oder Kolerin Sohn.

44 Leopold Haller Mrichen
Hallers Sohn von der forstmaisterin oder Kolerin sohn.

51

Lorentz Raimund Wilhelm Rietmuds
Sohn geborn von der Vintzingin.

48. Steffan Letzel Jobsten
Letzel vnd der Hallerin
Sohn.

Hannß Starck VI Starcker Sohn von der Trachtin erzäugt.

52. Wilhelm Hirschvogel Ulrich Hirschvogel und der Koptin Sohn.

Hannß Misat Hanußen Misat Sohn geborn von der Knoblin.

54 Carl Holtzschuer Carl Holtz-schuer Sohn von der Pirts-inngne.

Sebaldt Elbanager Sebalden
Elbanagers Sohn von der
Pömmerin.

56. Petter Zolner Gerhart
Zollners Son von der
Grundtherzin.

Albian Hegner Albian Hegner
vnd der Elwangerin Sohn.

58. Jörg Derrer Anthoni Derrer
vnd der Schnöttin Sohn.

Baptist Starcks.

Ao 1539.

Reinhard Leus.

62.

63.

Sigmund Meüsing A° 1539

Darnus Stromer·

64.

Albrecht Schünc

Wogst Menzni. A°: 1546.

69.

Moris Printn. d.º 1561. Wilhem Printn.

75.

76.

77.

76.

79.

80.

81.

A + o.
82

83

84.

85.

86.

87.

88.

89.

90.

91.

92.

93.

94.

95.

96.

100.

119.

125.

126.

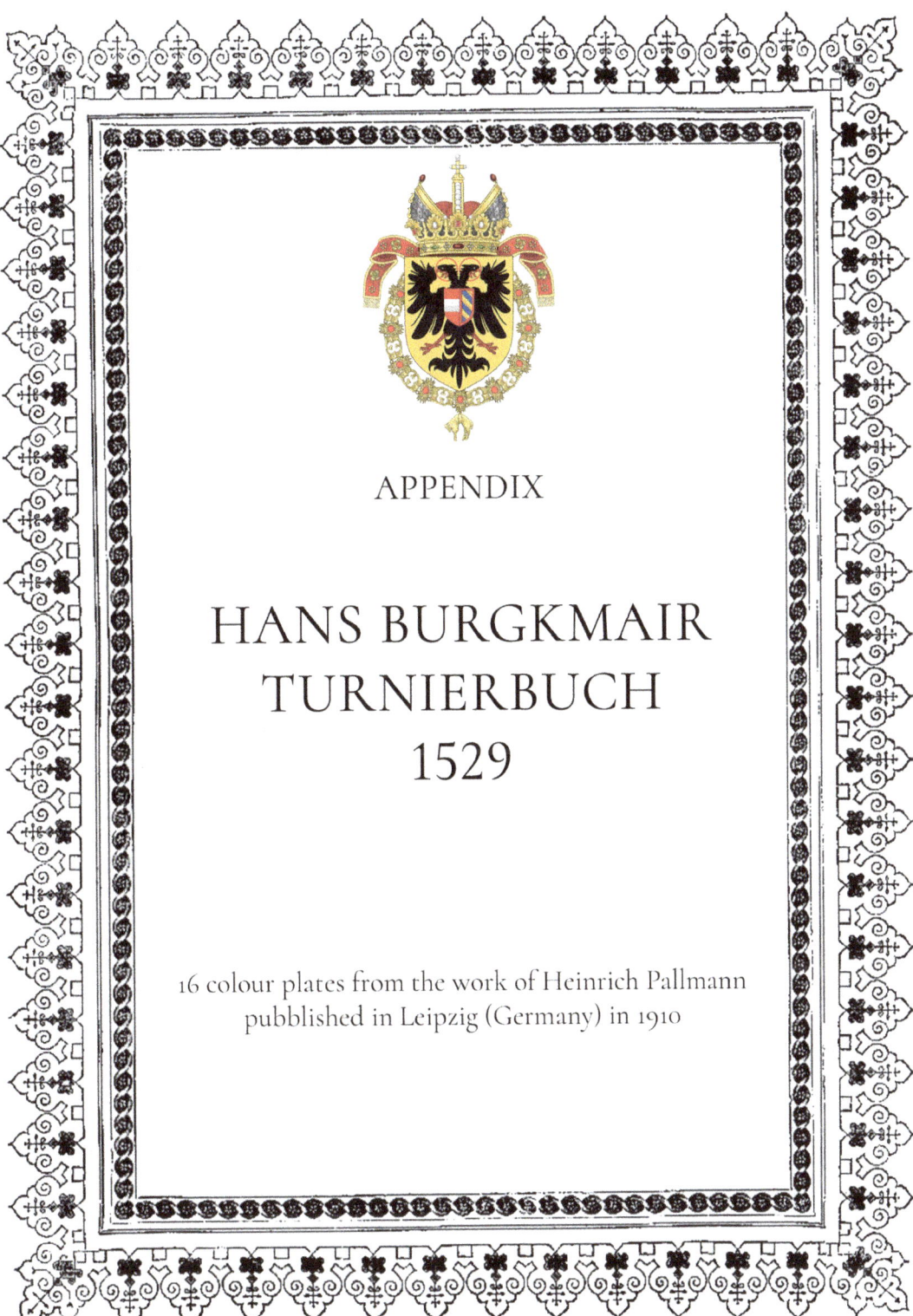

APPENDIX

HANS BURGKMAIR
TURNIERBUCH
1529

16 colour plates from the work of Heinrich Pallmann
pubblished in Leipzig (Germany) in 1910

Dem durchleuchtigen hochgebornen fürsten vnd herren/
herren Wilhalm pfaltzgrauen bey Rein/ herr Jogen in ob-
ern vnd nidern Bayrn/ ꝛc seinem gnedigen herren dise
weylend kaiser Maximilians hochloblichster gedechtnus/
verordnet vnd angeben gestäche/ vmd Rennspill durch
hannsen Burckmair den elltern maller zü Augspurg/ erst-
lich in verzaichnus genomen/ gemache/ vmd in diss werck
gericht/ hat hanns Burckmayr der junger vnderthenig-
lich zügestellt vnd vberantwort/ demselben sein fürst-
lichen ghaden/ sich daneben diemütigclich thüt beuelhen/

IMP.CÆS.MAXIMILIANI·AVG.
PRAEEXERCITAMENTA
MILITARIA

Herr Anthoni vonn Yfan
Thurmermaister /

Zue Augspurg.

Thurniever zu Roß

Caesar Zu augspurg

Steyr
Caesar

Brandenburg

Herr wolffganng vonm Polhaym
Xnn vnnd gestaichmaister

Zue Funsprugg

Das Tewtsch gestuch

Vestäch in dan hochen dückh Zue Grätz
In der Steyrmark beschehen.

Kay. Maximilian

Zue Innsprugg

Das Gestäch Im bam harnasch
mit lidrm deckenn/

Habspurg

Alt Badenn.

103

Zue Augspurg.

Das wellsch Rennen in den Armeten

Montfort

Sonnenberg

Das Bünndt Fannen

Werdenberg

Rechberg

Das geschifft Tartfchen Rennen

Pemßham   Ryndorff

Das geschifft scheyben rennen

Losenstain

frūntsperg

D H

Das pfannen Zennen

Das felld Rennen den burmdt
mit stehlin geliger.

Fürstenberg

Falckenstain

Zue   Augspurg.

Pennen mit fest anzügen / mit
wüllin Frennden /

H. Jacob von Ems   herr Casspar Mümtzer

SOME MEDIEVAL BOOKS ALREADY PUBLISHED

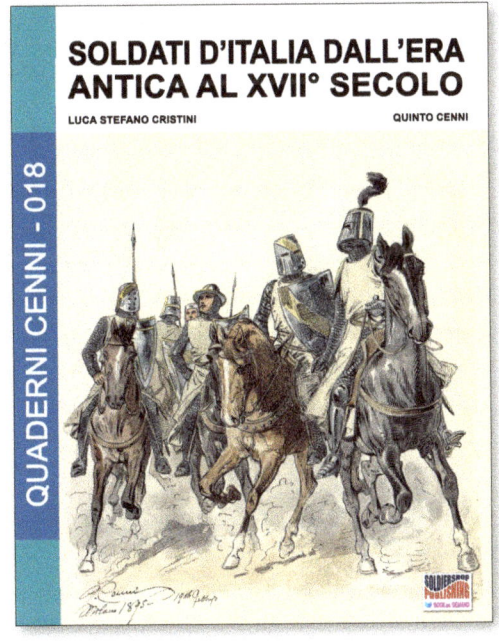

CRISTINI EDITORE

SOLDIERSHOP PUBLISHING